WINCHESTER

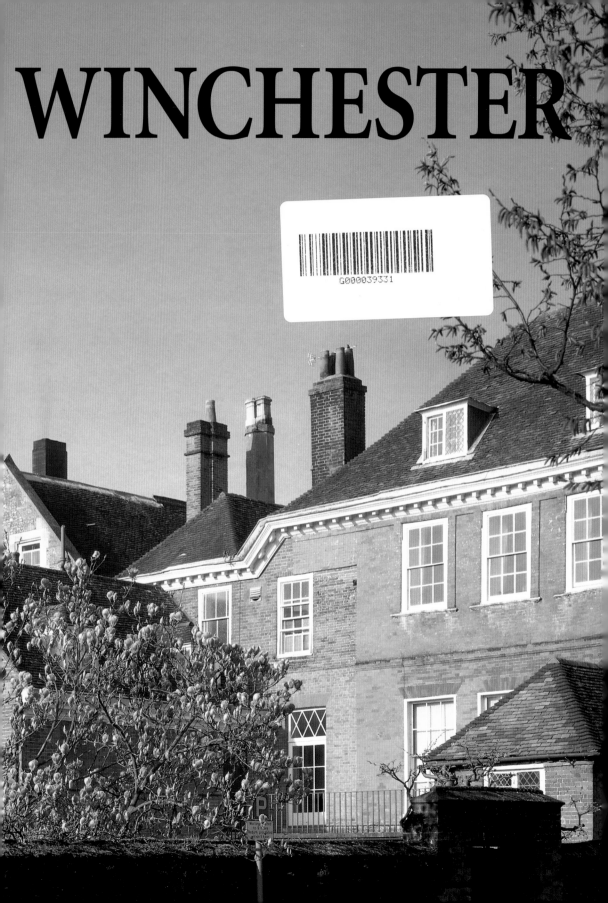

Situated amidst the chalk downs of Hampshire, in the green valley of the river Itchen, Winchester basks in an atmosphere of beauty, antiquity and calm. Its fascinating architecture and history greets you at every turn, while at its heart the venerable Norman cathedral presides. It is hard to believe that a city with such an air of peace can ever have been the site of dispute and destruction, but this it has been on many occasions in its history, losing priceless treasures and marvellous buildings to fanatical Reformers and zealous Parliamentarians, among others.

It is the bishops of Winchester to whom we owe much of what we see in the city today – Wolvesey Palace where many monarchs lodged, the Hospital of St Cross in the water meadows, Winchester College and the cathedral itself.

For hundreds of years hordes of pilgrims in need of help and healing were attracted to the shrine of St Swithun, to whom the cathedral priory was dedicated. Visitors to Winchester today are allured by a city richly endowed by the skilled hand of man and the generosity of nature.

c.410
Romans abandon the city.
648
Foundation of Old Minster by King Cenwalh of Wessex.

871–8
Alfred is crowned king and fortifies Winchester against Viking attack.
901–3
New Minster founded by King Alfred's son and Nunnaminster by King Alfred's widow.

1066–7
Winchester surrenders to William the Conqueror, who builds castle and royal palace.

2000–100 BC
Bronze Age activity; Iron Age settlements.
AD 43–70
Romans use Iron Age enclosure at Oram's Arbour and create capital town of Venta Belgarum.

859
Bishop Swithun constructs bridge over Itchen and walls around Close.
862
Bishop Swithun dies and is buried outside Old Minster.

964
Old Minster reformed as Benedictine priory of St Swithun by Bishop Ethelwold.
late 970s
Bishop Ethelwold builds bishop's palace at Wolvesey.

1079
Bishop Walkelin begins present cathedral.

1110
Monks of New Minster move to Hyde Abbey, taking bones of King Alfred.
1387
Building of Winchester College begun.

1348–51
Black Death kills more than half Winchester's citizens.

1554
Queen Mary Tudor and Philip of Spain marry at the cathedral.
1642
Parliamentarians ransack cathedral and bombard castle.

1651
Except for Great Hall, castle is destroyed.
1666
Plague hits Winchester, pits dug south of St Catherine's Hill.

1901
Statue of King Alfred erected in Broadway.
1906–1912
Cathedral underpinned with help of diver William Walker.

1136
Hospital of St Cross founded by Bishop Henry of Blois.
1235
Henry III builds Great Hall as part of castle modernization.

1446
Hospital of St Cross refounded by Cardinal Beaufort.
1538
Henry VIII dissolves city's three monasteries.

1680s
Bishop Morley builds new palace at Wolvesey.
1744
City Mill is rebuilt.
1817
Jane Austen dies in Winchester.

1993
Cathedral Visitors' Centre opened by Her Majesty the Queen.
1994
M3 cut through Twyford Down, amid much controversy and demonstration.

The Broadway

From the east end of the Broadway the bronze statue of Alfred the Great, Winchester's heroic Saxon king, watches imperiously over the city which he rebuilt after the Dark Ages as a defence site against the Vikings, and made the capital of Wessex.

KING ALFRED THE GREAT

Possibly Winchester's best-known landmark, Hamo Thorneycroft's immense bronze statue of the Saxon King Alfred was erected in 1901 to mark the millenary of his death. The day of its unveiling was declared a public holiday, and huge crowds attended to celebrate the much-loved King of Wessex who had successfully held back the invading Vikings and promoted the education and religious instruction of his people. Alfred was buried in Old Minster (▷ 6) in 899, and his ghost is said to have haunted the church until his body was transferred to New Minster (▷ 6), founded by his son, Edward the Elder.

ABBEY HOUSE

In 1538 most of Winchester's monastic buildings were dissolved and demolished at Henry VIII's command. In the mid 18th century a fine town house with formal gardens was built on the site of the Nunnaminster, and called Abbey House. The Tudor Gothic-style frontage was added in the early 19th century. Abbey House is now the official residence of the Mayor of Winchester.

ABBEY GARDENS

This attractive public park has a stream running through, and a playground for young children.

NUNNAMINSTER

The Nunnaminster was one of Saxon Winchester's three royal monasteries. Founded in *c.*903 by King Alfred's widow, Queen Ealhswith, the nuns' minster occupied a site south of the Broadway. Remains of Ealhswith's timber church can be seen in Abbey Passage.

Nunnaminster remains

GUILDHALL

The flamboyant Gothic-revival Guildhall, opened in 1873, is now used for public events and conferences. It also houses the Tourist Information Centre, a restaurant and café, and a gallery exhibiting a changing programme of contemporary art.

Guildhall

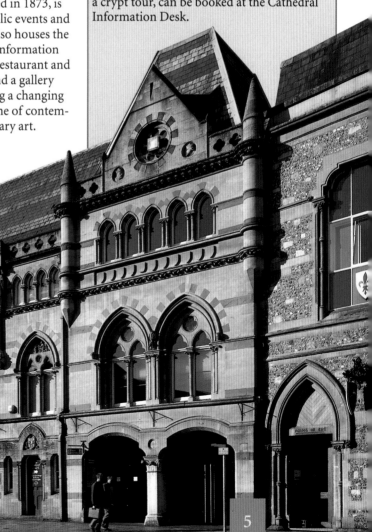

WALKS AND TOURS

Guided tours: A 1½-hour tour with a Blue Badge Guide begins at the Tourist Information Centre, where you can buy your ticket. If you are with a group, you may need to book ahead. Many special interest tours are available.

Self-guided walks: A range of leaflets is available at the Tourist Information Centre.

Winchester Ghost Walk will acquaint you with the horrors of Viking raids, tortures and plague pits. Phone 01962 881957 for details.

Winchester College guided tours take place three times a day from April to September. Phone the Porter's Lodge on 01962 621227.

Cathedral tours, including a tower tour for ages 12–70 or, when the weather has been dry, a crypt tour, can be booked at the Cathedral Information Desk.

The Cathedral

Winchester's mighty cathedral was started in 1079, nine years after the Norman Conquest. Walkelin, a Norman bishop appointed by William the Conqueror, was charged with replacing the Anglo-Saxon Old Minster with a huge new Romanesque cathedral. In 1093, when it was half built, the monks visited Old Minster for the last time to collect the relics of their patron, St Swithun (▷ 23), and transfer them in solemn procession to the new cathedral. Despite numerous modifications, much of the cathedral's Norman architecture can still be seen, and bones of many early Saxon monarchs and bishops are still housed there, in mortuary chests.

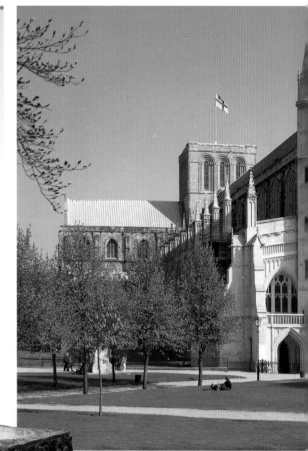

OLD MINSTER

The first minster church was built more or less on the site of the present cathedral in 648 by a Christian king, Cenwalh of Wessex. It soon became a cathedral where many of the kings of Wessex, and later of all England, were buried. In 964 Bishop Ethelwold reformed Old Minster as a Benedictine monastery known as St Swithun's Priory. The monastery survived for the next 600 years, but when the new Norman cathedral was built in 1093 Old Minster church was demolished. The lines of its foundations are marked out in brick to the north of the present cathedral.

NEW MINSTER

New Minster was founded by Edward the Elder in 901. It was built uncomfortably close to Old Minster, only a few feet to its north, and the remains of King Alfred (▷ 4) were reburied there. In 1110 the monks moved out to Hyde Abbey (▷ 19), taking Alfred's bones with them.

MARBLE FONT

The 12th-century black Tournai marble font shows two miracles from the legends of St Nicholas, the patron saint of sailors and children. On one side the saint produces three bags of gold as marriage dowries for the daughters of an impoverished nobleman, while on another St Nicholas raises to life three boys who have been murdered by a wicked landlord.

THE TOWER

In 1107 Bishop Walkelin's Norman tower collapsed. This catastrophe was blamed by many on the wicked King William Rufus (William II), who had been buried beneath it seven years previously. The new tower was built with great caution, as can be seen from its very solid appearance.

Winchester Cathedral

JANE AUSTEN'S GRAVE

The grave of Jane Austen (▷ 22), on the north side of the nave, bears an affectionate tribute to her delightful personality, but makes no mention of her skill as a novelist. Her writing is cited on the brass wall tablet nearby, paid for with the proceeds of her first biography. The memorial window above it depicts, among others, King David, writer of the psalms.

TRANSEPTS

The north and south transepts give the best idea of Bishop Walkelin's great Norman cathedral, built in three storeys.

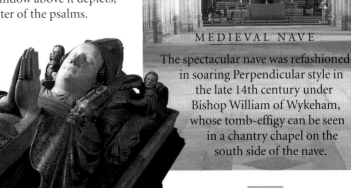

MEDIEVAL NAVE

The spectacular nave was refashioned in soaring Perpendicular style in the late 14th century under Bishop William of Wykeham, whose tomb-effigy can be seen in a chantry chapel on the south side of the nave.

The Cathedral

Crypt

GREAT SCREEN

During the reign of Elizabeth I, Bishop Horne, opposed to all forms of idol-worship, pulled down and smashed all the original statues from this splendid late 15th-century reredos. The current statues are 19th-century replacements.

WILLIAM WALKER

By the beginning of the 20th century the east end of the cathedral, built on a raft of beech logs on marshy ground, was subsiding and in danger of collapse. The high water table necessitated employing a deep sea diver, William Walker, who worked under the foundations in murky, dark water for over five years, digging out the rotting timber and laying firm foundations of bags of cement concrete. He is commemorated by a bronze statue in the retrochoir.

NORMAN CRYPT

Situated beneath the east end of the cathedral, the beautiful and secret Norman crypt often floods, and the statue by Antony Gormley, 'Sound II', was designed specifically to stand in the water.

CHOIR STALLS

The magnificent choir stalls, made in about 1308, depict a lively enchanted forest. In these stalls the monks of St Swithun's Priory would sing their numerous daily services, resting upon their misericords (▷ 17).

IN HONOUR OF WILLIAM WALKER THE DIVER WHO SAVED THIS CATHEDRAL WITH HIS TWO HANDS 1906–1912

RETROCHOIR

Built in the 13th century to accommodate the crowds of pilgrims to the shrine of St Swithun (▷ 23), the retrochoir has the largest surviving area of medieval floor tiles in the country. At the centre of the retro-choir screen may be seen the Holy Hole, a low tunnel which allowed pilgrims to crawl beneath a platform on which Swithun's bones were displayed in order to get closer to their curative powers.

PARLIAMENTARIAN ATTACK

In December 1642 Parliamentarian soldiers burst through the west doors of the cathedral, some of them on horseback, and created havoc, vandalizing the high altar, throwing out priceless manuscripts and smashing the medieval glass with the precious bones of Saxon saints and kings.

STUDY TO BE QUIET

THE FISHERMEN'S CHAPEL

The beautiful oak altar (▷ 16) and the fluid wooden benches create a rural, watery atmosphere in this peaceful chapel, properly called the St John the Evangelist and the Fishermen Apostle's Chapel, where Izaak Walton, fisherman and author of *The Compleat Angler*, was buried in 1683. The Fishermen's Window depicts Walton reading by the river Itchen, with St Catherine's Hill behind him.

BOY CHORISTERS

Cathedral choristers selected through voice trials are awarded scholarships to The Pilgrims' School in the Close (▷ 11). Once 'dubbed' full choristers, they take part in a busy programme of cathedral services, recordings, concerts, broadcasts and tours, leading a demanding yet rewarding life in a world-famous choir.

LIBRARY AND TRIFORIUM GALLERY

The priceless Winchester Bible, on permanent display in the Library, is an exquisite example of 12th-century illumination, for which the 'Winchester School' was renowned. The gallery's exhibits include some of the beautiful original statues of the Great Screen, and fragments from the 13th-century shrine of St Swithun (▷ 23).

The Close

Once the site of the domestic buildings of St Swithun's Priory, the beautiful Cathedral Close seems to retain the peaceful atmosphere of the monastery, with evidence of its existence in several of the buildings.

THE DEANERY

Still fronted by its 13th-century vaulted porch, the Deanery, once the Prior's lodgings, was largely rebuilt in the 17th century after damage during the Civil War. The red brick Long Gallery was added in 1671 so that Winchester's frequent visitor Charles II could entertain in fitting style. The hall on the left is 15th-century.

NORMAN CHAPTER HOUSE

The Norman arches of the chapter house, the business centre of the priory, are one of the few remaining traces of the monastery buildings that were swept away after the Dissolution.

Visitors' Centre

Chapter House ruins

CATHEDRAL VISITORS' CENTRE

Continuing the Benedictine tradition of hospitality, the Visitors' Centre Refectory gives a warm welcome to its guests. The Cathedral Shop, which incorporates a 17th-century coach house, sells souvenirs and an excellent range of gifts.

PILGRIMS' HALL

The Pilgrims' Hall, adjacent to The Pilgrims' School, is traditionally believed to have been the priory guest-house, where pilgrims to St Swithun's shrine (▷ 23) would have gathered for food and shelter. The flint-rubble walled hall, open to the public, has the oldest surviving hammer-beam roof in England, dating from possibly as early as *c*.1290.

THE PILGRIMS' SCHOOL

This prep school, opened in 1931, continues the Close's tradition of pre-eminent education which began with the Saxon 'Alta Schola'. Based around a late 17th-century house, the school uses some of the Close's oldest buildings in which to educate the Cathedral Choristers (▷ 9), College Quiristers (▷ 25), and a large number of 'Commoners'.

PRIORY STABLES

The fine early 16th-century timber-framed building opposite St Swithun's Gate, once the Close's stable block, is now a part of The Pilgrims' School.

CHEYNEY COURT

One of the most photographed sights in Winchester, it was in this late 16th-century building that the bishop held his court over the Soke (▷ 28–29).

Cheyney Court

DEAN GARNIER'S GARDEN

Named after Thomas Garnier, Dean of Winchester from 1840 and distinguished horticulturist, this tranquil garden was created on the site of the monks' dormitory and designed to reflect the architecture of the cathedral.

PRIORY GATE

The 16th-century gate, with its nail-studded doors and little inset pedestrian gate, is surmounted by a tiny house, originally intended for the cathedral organist.

The Square

Once the site of a cattle market with open stalls, the L-shaped Square is a charmingly unspoilt corner of Winchester, where specialist shops jostle for attention with pubs and restaurants. Nothing remains above ground of the royal palace which was built here in 1069 by William the Conqueror, spanning the area of the Square and the Cathedral Yard.

TOWN CRIER

There has been a town crier in Winchester at least since 1285, when he was responsible for keeping the peace and preventing fires. Today's town crier has no such responsibilities, but maintains an ancient tradition while presenting a light-hearted slant on local events.

City Museum

ST LAWRENCE-IN-THE-SQUARE

Hemmed in by offices and shops, the little 15th-century church of St Lawrence is thought to stand on the site of a chapel of the New Minster (▷ 6), or of William's royal palace. A rather macabre feature of the church's history is that a bell was tolled here before public executions in the square, but it is also to this church that each new bishop comes for private prayer before his enthronement in the cathedral ((▷ 6–9).

ST LAWRENCE PASSAGE

On a chimney breast in St Lawrence Passage are some small patterned stones of a horseshoe design, believed to have been salvaged from the royal palace that once stood here.

Christ's Hospital

CHRIST'S HOSPITAL, SYMONDS STREET

Peter Symonds, a wealthy Winchester textile merchant, founded this almshouse in 1607 for the maintenance of six old men, one matron and four boys. He also provided for one scholar at Oxford and one at Cambridge.

CITY MUSEUM

On the site of the old Market House, this intriguing museum contains important exhibits illustrating the archaeology and history of Winchester, including a superb section of 2nd-century Roman mosaic pavement, and 4th-century wall-paintings.

High Street

When the Romans arrived in Winchester they built a military fort at Oram's Arbour, making use of an enclosure of the Iron Age tribe, the Belgae. Within 25 years they had founded a major town which they called Venta Belgarum – the market place of the Belgae. Venta flourished, and within its walls arose a forum, basilica, temple and fine houses, and a grid of streets based on the main east–west road, from which today's High Street originates.

OLD GUILDHALL

The Old Guildhall (Lloyds Bank) was rebuilt in 1713 after a visit by Queen Anne, in the hope that Winchester might once again become a royal city. It was at this time that the statue of Queen Anne and the great bracket clock, of which the present one is a replica, were added. At 8 o'clock each weekday evening a curfew bell tolls from the bell tower – a tradition that dates from Norman times.

Anna Regina
Anne Pacifico
· 1713 ·

THE PENTICE

THE PENTICE

This attractive covered way in the High Street was created when the upper floors of the 16th-century timber-framed houses were extended. It was once called the King's Mint after the 13th-century royal mint that had operated there until 1279.

GOD BEGOT HOUSE

The present God Begot House dates from 1558, but it stands on the site of the ancient manor of God Begot which Queen Emma, widow of King Canute, bequeathed to St Swithun's Priory in 1052. The limits of the manor provided a sanctuary where anyone who had broken the law could shelter. Citizens who entered God Begot with intent to arrest or assault one of its inhabitants faced excommunication, while God Begotters had to pay a large sum to gain freedom of the city. Trade between the two factions was strictly forbidden. A passage alongside the house leads to 'The Royal Oak', which claims to be the oldest bar in England.

ANTIQUES MARKET

A fascinating variety of small antiques, accessories and clothing is sold from numerous stalls at this indoor market in Kings Walk.

THE MARKET

Winchester's flourishing market takes place from Wednesday through to Saturday selling food and a variety of household goods. Flowers are sold throughout the week.

BUTTERCROSS

In 1770 Winchester's decorative 15th-century city cross was almost sold to a local landowner who fancied it as a garden decoration, but heated protests by citizens ensured that the cross stayed. Radically restored in 1865, the Buttercross is still seen as the centre of Winchester, and is used by many as a meeting place.

THE BROOKS

The Brooks shopping centre was built on part of the area called the Brooks which takes its name from the watercourses that have crossed it for thousands of years. These streams still flow under the ground. The site was excavated, and Roman and medieval finds are displayed in The Brooks Experience, incorporated in the shopping centre.

Birds and Beasts

It is fitting that Winchester, a city in the heart of the country-side, should be scattered with decorative birds and beasts of all kinds, who have seemingly crept from the water meadows and the downs into the historic streets and buildings to become immortalized in the city's fabric.

A fine falcon decorates the fountain in Queen Eleanor's Garden (▷ 21), outside the Great Hall.

Beware! Ducks crossing! – a necessary road sign in watery Winchester.

Situated near the Westgate (▷ 18), the *Horse and Rider* is a 1975 bronze sculpture by Elizabeth Frink.

Swimming fish adorn the beautiful oak altar of the chapel of St John the Evangelist and the Fishermen Apostles in the cathedral (▷ 9). The altar, made in 1995 by Peter Eugene Ball, was carved from an oak tree struck down in a storm.

Birds decorate this 10th-century copper-alloy strap-end on display in the City Museum (▷ 13).

This musical monkey is just one of the fantastic creatures of the enchanted forest that decorates the cathedral's superb choir stalls (▷ 8).

A miscellany of grotesque and amusing creatures decorates the medieval misericords in the choir stalls of the cathedral (▷ 8) and college chapel (▷ 25). A misericord is a little ledge, beneath the fold-up seat, on which a weary monk or college boy could rest while standing through the hours of mass.

The Hampshire Hog is a life-size bronze sculpture by David Kemp, commissioned by Hampshire County Council in 1989 and adopted as its insignia. It stands in front of the Council Offices near the Westgate (▷ 18).

Depicted on the cathedral's Great Screen (▷ 8) is the hermit St Giles, who made a companion of a hind and lived on her milk. One day the hind, finding herself stalked by a hunter, sought the protection of St Giles, causing him to be injured and crippled by the arrow that was intended for her. St Giles became known as the protector of nursing mothers and the patron saint of cripples. A chapel dedicated to the saint once stood on St Giles' Hill (▷ 29).

The Westgate

At the top of the High Street stands the impressive Westgate, a fortified medieval gateway built on the site of the original Roman gate.

WESTGATE

The Westgate is one of the two surviving medieval gateways that were once an integral part of the city wall. Originally built in the 12th century and later remodelled, the west face was added in the 14th century to defend the city against threatened invasion from France. The openings below the parapet on the west face of the gate were for dropping ammunition such as rocks, oil or even boiling lead on potential invaders. The loops below the shields were designed for primitive hand-held cannons, and the slots in the gateway arch held a portcullis. The little room above the arch, originally a guardroom, served as a debtors' prison from the 16th to the 18th century, and is now a museum.

WESTGATE MUSEUM

The Westgate's little museum has a fascinating collection of exhibits, including weights and measures and a set of gruesome gibbeting irons. The Tudor ceiling was transferred from Winchester College (▷ 24–25), where it had decorated a warden's room to celebrate the wedding of Mary I and Philip of Spain in 1554. The walls are scratched with graffiti from the time that it was a prison, the earliest inscription dating from 1597. There is a fine view from the roof, which is open to the public.

Westgate

LITTLE TREATS IN WINCHESTER

- Choral Evensong in the cathedral (▷ 6–9) every term-time evening except Wednesday.
- Hearing the cathedral bells toll in the Close (▷ 10–11) on Sunday morning.
- A lunch break in the Cathedral Refectory (▷ 10).
- Standing over the mill race at the City Mill (▷ 29).
- A browse around the Kings Walk antiques market (▷ 15).
- A drink at the famous Wykeham Arms (▷ 23).
- A leisurely stroll in the beautiful water meadows (▷ 26).
- The panoramic views from St Giles' Hill (▷ 29) or St Catherine's Hill (▷ 26).
- A quiet moment in the peaceful 'Fishermen's Chapel' in the cathedral (▷ 9).

Westgate's rooftop view

HYDE ABBEY

By 1110 the site around the cathedral had become overcrowded, and Henry I ordered the monks of New Minster (▷ 6) to move to a new abbey at Hyde, outside the north gate. The monks took with them the remains of King Alfred (▷ 4), his wife Queen Ealhswith and his son Edward the Elder, and buried them in front of the high altar. Hyde Abbey became a place of pilgrimage and prospered throughout the medieval period, but in 1538 fell victim to Henry VIII's commissioners. Now only its 15th-century gatehouse remains.

MILITARY MUSEUMS

Winchester's military museums present the history of five famous regiments of the British Army. The museums of the Light Infantry, the Gurkhas, the King's Royal Hussars and the Royal Green Jackets are located within Peninsular Barracks, and the Royal Hampshire Regiment museum is in Southgate Street.

The Great Hall

One of the finest medieval buildings in the country, Henry III's Great Hall, dating from 1235, is all that remains of Winchester's castle, though fragments of the foundations of William the Conqueror's original castle can be seen in Castle Yard.

WINCHESTER CASTLE

In November 1066 Winchester surrendered without fight to William the Conqueror. Within weeks of his coronation he had ordered the construction of a castle at Winchester, which was to be the seat of government under the early Norman kings. It was almost completely rebuilt during the long reign of Henry III (1216–72), and with its magnificent Great Hall was one of the finest castles in the land. But after an extensive fire in 1302 it ceased to be used as a royal residence, and monarchs lodged at the bishop's palace of Wolvesey (▷ 28). During the Civil War the castle was besieged by the Royalists until it was captured by Cromwell's Parliamentary forces in 1645. Six years later the castle was demolished, but the Great Hall was kept as a venue for assemblies and county assizes.

THE GREAT HALL

To get a realistic picture of Henry III's Great Hall, visitors must imagine walls decorated with patterns and coats of arms, and adornments of large pictures and statues. Until the 1970s the Great Hall was used for the administration of justice. It was here, in 1603, that Sir Walter Raleigh was condemned to death, and in 1685 that the ferocious Judge Jeffreys sentenced Alice Lisle to be beheaded for concealing two refugees after the Battle of Sedgemoor. Today the hall is used for major ceremonial occasions, particularly royal visits.

THE ROUND TABLE

King Arthur's Round Table has hung in the Great Hall for over 600 years. It was made in the 13th century, about 700 years after Arthur's death, though legend has it that it was made by the wizard Merlin. The table was painted during the reign of Henry VIII, depicting Arthur in Tudor robes, and with the face of Henry VIII.

QUEEN VICTORIA

The great bronze statue of Queen Victoria was commissioned for her Golden Jubilee in 1897. Back to back with the queen is Britannia, and Victory flies over the globe in her hand.

QUEEN ELEANOR'S GARDEN

This reconstruction of a medieval garden, based on an illustration from a 14th-century manuscript, was created in 1986. The garden is named after two Queen Eleanors of England.

ROYAL PALACE

Charles II visited Winchester frequently for the horse racing, and when he commissioned Christopher Wren to build a huge royal palace on the site of the old castle it seemed as if Winchester might regain its former royal importance. But the palace was left unfinished and was burned down in 1894.

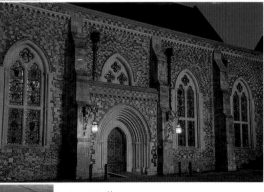

Great Hall

Just outside the cathedral gate stands the Kingsgate, one of the two medieval gateways of Roman origin that survive in Winchester. It is surmounted by the lovely little church of St Swithun, and stands close to the house where Jane Austen spent her final days.

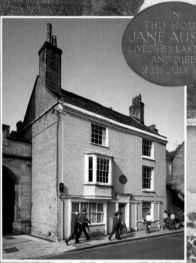

JANE AUSTEN'S HOUSE

The private house at No. 8 College Street that has become known as 'Jane Austen's House' is where the great English novelist lived for the last six weeks of her life. Jane had spent the previous eight years living with her mother and sister, Cassandra, at their home in Chawton (▷ 30), where she had written or revised most of her novels, including *Pride and Prejudice* and *Emma*. But Jane became ill, and in May 1817 took up lodgings here with Cassandra in order to be near to the doctor who was treating her. Jane died of Addison's Disease on 18 July, aged 41. Her funeral was held in the cathedral, and she is buried in the north aisle of the nave (▷ 7).

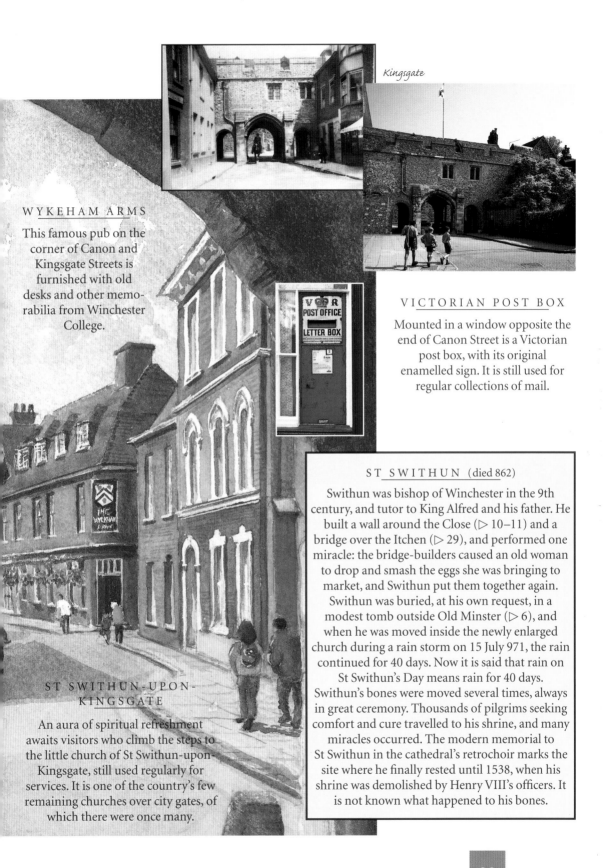

Kingsgate

WYKEHAM ARMS

This famous pub on the corner of Canon and Kingsgate Streets is furnished with old desks and other memorabilia from Winchester College.

VICTORIAN POST BOX

Mounted in a window opposite the end of Canon Street is a Victorian post box, with its original enamelled sign. It is still used for regular collections of mail.

ST SWITHUN-UPON-KINGSGATE

An aura of spiritual refreshment awaits visitors who climb the steps to the little church of St Swithun-upon-Kingsgate, still used regularly for services. It is one of the country's few remaining churches over city gates, of which there were once many.

ST SWITHUN (died 862)

Swithun was bishop of Winchester in the 9th century, and tutor to King Alfred and his father. He built a wall around the Close ($\triangleright$ 10–11) and a bridge over the Itchen ($\triangleright$ 29), and performed one miracle: the bridge-builders caused an old woman to drop and smash the eggs she was bringing to market, and Swithun put them together again. Swithun was buried, at his own request, in a modest tomb outside Old Minster ($\triangleright$ 6), and when he was moved inside the newly enlarged church during a rain storm on 15 July 971, the rain continued for 40 days. Now it is said that rain on St Swithun's Day means rain for 40 days. Swithun's bones were moved several times, always in great ceremony. Thousands of pilgrims seeking comfort and cure travelled to his shrine, and many miracles occurred. The modern memorial to St Swithun in the cathedral's retrochoir marks the site where he finally rested until 1538, when his shrine was demolished by Henry VIII's officers. It is not known what happened to his bones.

Winchester College

Bishop William of Wykeham started Winchester College in 1387 to prepare 70 needy scholars for his recently founded New College, in Oxford, in order to produce well-educated priests at a time when so many had been lost to the Black Death. He could not have imagined that his school would be flourishing, and using most of its original buildings, some 600 years later.

OUTER GATE

The College Street gatehouse of what was originally called St Mary College is adorned with a beautiful statue of the Virgin and Child. In the vault of the gateway a carved stone face seems to smile at you as you enter and frown on you as you leave.

CHAMBER COURT

Boys used the washing place on the right of this fine medieval quadrangle every day, whatever the season, right up until the middle of the last century.

THE TRUSTY SERVANT

This intriguing 16th-century picture displayed in Trusty Servant Passage proclaims all the attributes of the ideal manservant, and bears the school motto, 'Manners Makyth Man'.

The Trusty Servant

GUIDED TOURS

A guided tour (▷ 5) will take you to further fascinating parts of the college: the 1395 Old Cloisters enclosing a chantry chapel, the building called School which is optimistically attributed to Christopher Wren, the beautiful and inspiring War Cloister and the Scholars' Dining Hall.

COLLEGE CHAPEL

Consecrated in *c.*1394, the beautiful chapel has undergone many changes, though the original ornate roof remains. Some medieval woodwork is preserved in the misericords (▷ 17). The precious, soft-coloured medieval stained glass to be seen in the south-west corner was recovered after being disposed of in the 19th century. Services are sung by the college choir which includes, by long-standing tradition, Wykeham's 16 young 'Quiristers', who are educated at The Pilgrims' School (▷ 11).

COLLEGE LIFE IN HISTORY

The Wykehamists of the past rebelled several times against the disproportionate discipline, frequent beatings and poor food. In 1793 they pulled up cobble-stones from Chamber Court, took them up into the tower and threw them down on the staff below. The college has been well-known in the past for its spartan conditions: right up until 1930 the boys went to bed by candlelight, and until 1961 they bathed in tin baths of cold water.

COLLEGE NOTIONS

Winchester College's strange traditions contribute to its success, not least its quirky vocabulary, called 'notions'. Prep (homework) time is called 'toytime' and the desks at which they do it, 'toys'. A bicycle is a 'bogle' and the WC is a 'foricas'. The expression 'going circum' for taking a walk probably derives from the time when exercise had to be taken round and round the cloisters.

Water Meadows and St Cross

One of the great pleasures of a visit to Winchester is a walk, in the footsteps of the poet Keats, through the verdant water meadows of the Itchen, to St Cross, where the medieval almshouse welcomes you with unspoilt calm.

ST CATHERINE'S HILL

Rising beyond the water meadows is the beautiful, gently rounded top of St Catherine's Hill, where once stood an Iron Age fort. The view from the top is the finest in the city, and children enjoy the extraordinary miz-maze, possibly cut as a penitential device where blind-folded monks would crawl.

Water meadows and St Catherine's Hill

JOHN KEATS (1795–1821)

During a two-month stay in Winchester in 1819, Keats' daily walk past the cathedral and the College, and through the water meadows to St Cross, was the inspiration for his ode *To Autumn*:

…Season of mists and mellow fruitfulness,

Close bosom-friend of the maturing sun;

Conspiring with him how to load and bless

With fruit the vines that round the thatch-eves run…

BROTHERS

St Cross Hospital is still home to 25 brothers, those of the original foundation dressing in a black gown with a badge of the Jerusalem Cross, and Beaufort's brothers wearing red, with a cardinal's badge. They live in self-contained flats in Beaufort's original, tall-chimneyed lodgings on the west of the quadrangle.

ST CROSS HOSPITAL

The Hospital of St Cross has provided sheltered accommodation for elderly gentlemen since its foundation in 1136. Bishop Henry of Blois founded the hospital to provide for 'thirteen poor men, feeble and so reduced in strength that they can scarcely or not at all support themselves without other aid', stipulating that the establishment should also feed a hundred poor people each day. The hospital received a second foundation by Bishop Cardinal Beaufort in 1446 as the Almshouse of Noble Poverty, for people of noble birth who had fallen on hard times, and it is from this time that many of the existing buildings survive.

Brethren's Hall

BRETHREN'S HALL

The remarkable *c*.1350 Brethren's Hall, with its impressive chestnut-beamed roof, is periodically used for a brothers' celebratory feast – called a Gaudy Lunch.

St Cross Hospital

Brethren's lodgings

WAYFARER'S DOLE

An ancient rule of the charitable trust prescribed that travellers should be given bread and ale. Visitors today who request the 'Wayfarer's Dole' from the Porter will be given a morsel of bread and a small beaker of ale, and will be taking part in an 800-year-old tradition.

ST CROSS CHURCH

Started in about 1131 and a fine example of Transitional Norman architecture, this church was a point of departure for crusaders to the Holy Land. Originally thatched, the church has an area of medieval floor tiles, and saw-marks on the lectern bear testimony to its mutilation by Cromwell's troops.

Wolvesey and the Soke

Bishop Ethelwold built the first bishop's palace at Wolvesey a thousand years ago, and it is here that his palace has stood ever since. The area of town under the bishop's jurisdiction was known as the Soke.

WOLVESEY PALACE RUINS

The first bishop's palace on this site was built by the Anglo-Saxon Ethelwold in the late 970s. This was added to and eventually superseded by the large, medieval palace of Henry of Blois, bishop from 1129, and it is the ruins of this that we now see at Wolvesey. Winchester's medieval bishops wielded tremendous power from their fortified and moat-surrounded palace, and entertained many kings and queens. In 1554 a feast was held here for Mary I, before her marriage to Philip of Spain in the cathedral.

Wolvesey Palace ruins

NEW BISHOP'S PALACE

In the mid 17th century Bishop George Morley, having spent much money repairing the medieval palace, decided that it was not viable as a bishop's residence, and stripped it of materials to build a new Baroque palace. Neglect of this palace led to its decline and only one wing remains, which is now occupied by the present Bishop of Winchester.

OLD CHESIL RECTORY

This fine late medieval timber-framed building on Chesil Street is one of Winchester's oldest houses, dating from 1450.

Old Chesil Rectory

WEIRS WALK

From Wolvesey Palace to the City Bridge, between the clear-watered Itchen and the medieval city wall, runs the charming Weirs Walk. The City Bridge stands at an ancient river crossing place, the first bridge having been built by the 9th-century bishop, Swithun (▷ 23). A short way from the bridge stands the only remaining visible section of the city's Roman wall.

CITY MILL

The first mill on this site was built over 900 years ago, just outside the east gate of the city wall. Powered by the fast-flowing Itchen, it processed Hampshire's main agricultural products, grain and wool. The present mill, built in 1744, has been partly restored by the National Trust, and visitors can admire the master wheel, enjoy the dramatic mill-race, and visit the tiny island garden.

City Mill

ST GILES' HILL

The viewpoint at the top of St Giles' Hill, a short sign-posted climb from the Soke, offers superb panoramic views of the city. In the Middle Ages this was the site of the annual St Giles' Fair, one of the great fairs of Europe.

Out of Town Visits

Visitors wishing to explore the beautiful Hampshire countryside around Winchester will find dramatic hills, extensive woods and superb walks. The delightful small towns of Stockbridge, Alresford and Romsey are all within a short distance, as are many fascinating places to visit.

MARWELL ZOOLOGICAL PARK

Situated 5 miles south-east of Winchester at Owslebury, this spacious zoo, set in 100 acres of parkland, is home to a thousand rare and endangered species of wildlife. Visitors can enjoy the forest animal complex, the tropical house and Penguin World.

Watercress Lin

SIR HAROLD HILLIER GARDENS AND ARBORETUM

This beautiful 166-acre landscaped garden, 9 miles south-west of Winchester, features one of the finest collections of trees and shrubs in Britain.

MOTTISFONT ABBEY AND GARDEN

The walled garden of Mottisfont Abbey, set beside a tributary of the River Test, contains the National Trust's collection of old-fashioned roses. Mottisfont is 10 miles south-west of Winchester.

Mottisfont

JANE AUSTEN'S HOUSE AT CHAWTON

Jane Austen (▷ 22) lived the last eight years of her life at this delightful house in Chawton, near Alton, 15 miles east of Winchester, writing some of her great masterpieces. It is now a museum of her life, interests and work, surrounded by a pretty garden.

DANEBURY HILL FORT

Just beyond the town of Stockbridge, 10 miles west of Winchester, the impressive Iron Age settlement of Danebury, with its huge surrounding banks and ditches, is a wonderful place to walk and explore. Extensive excavations in recent years have revealed the life of a stable township with a rich culture.

WHITCHURCH SILK MILL

This working silk-weaving mill, situated on the River Test, uses antique machinery to produce high quality silk fabrics for interior design and costume drama productions. Whitchurch is 12 miles north of Winchester.

WATERCRESS LINE

The Mid-Hants steam railway, fondly known as the Watercress Line because of the watercress beds in the area, is a 10-mile line which runs through the Hampshire countryside from the charming town of Alresford, 8 miles east of Winchester.

BISHOP'S WALTHAM

Remains of the largest medieval palace of Winchester's powerful bishops can be seen at the delightful small town of Bishop's Waltham, 12 miles south-east of Winchester.

ROMSEY ABBEY

The small town of Romsey, 10 miles south-west of Winchester, is well worth a visit for its wonderful Norman Abbey, built mainly in the 12th century.

WINCHESTER FOR CHILDREN

Abbey Gardens (▷ 4), **Oram's Arbour** and **North Walls Park** have children's play equipment.

Intech, in Kings Road off Romsey Road, is an exciting hands-on technology exhibition with free admission.

The **cathedral** (▷ 6–9) offers a pictorial guide for children and observation trails.

Feed the ducks and watch the ducklings at **Weirs Walk** (▷ 29).

The Westgate Museum (▷ 18) offers brass rubbing and a History Detective Quiz.

St Giles' Hill (▷ 29) is ideal for ball games, kite flying, treasure trails and tracking games.

Hat Fair

The Hat Fair, held early in July each year, is a lively open-air festival full of wacky street entertainers and unusual stalls.

The miz-maze on **St Catherine's Hill** (▷ 26) is fascinating to children and adults alike.

Winnall Moors Nature Reserve, reached via Durngate Place or North Walls Park, is a beautiful area of unspoilt marshland and water meadows stretching along the river.

The Watercress Line (▷ 31) is a great experience for children, who will enjoy the Santa Specials at Christmas and the visits from Thomas the Tank Engine and Friends.

Marwell Zoo (▷ 30) has an area where children can touch the animals.

Paulton's Park, near Romsey, is a large leisure park with exciting rides for children, attractive gardens and exotic birds.

Intech

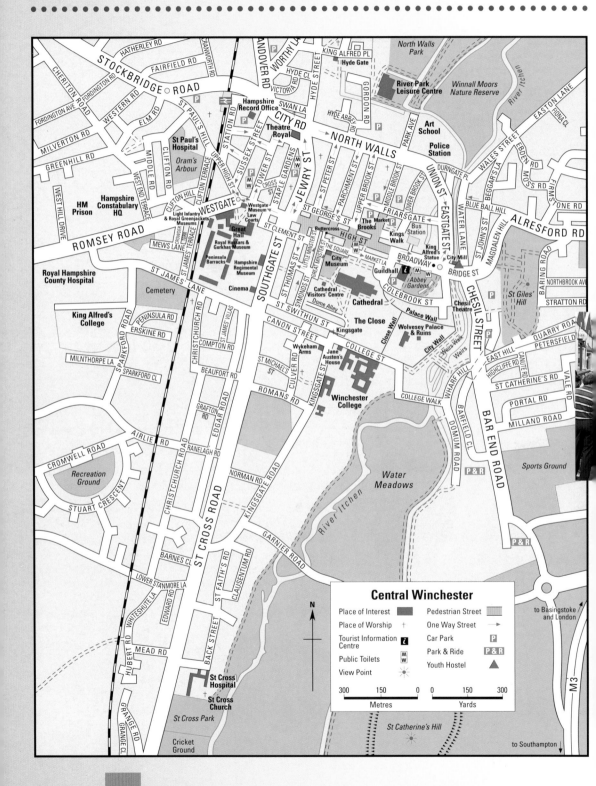

Central Winchester

Place of Interest		Pedestrian Street	
Place of Worship	†	One Way Street	→
Tourist Information Centre	*i*	Car Park	P
Public Toilets	M W	Park & Ride	P&R
View Point	☀	Youth Hostel	▲

300　　150　　0　　　0　　150　　300
Metres　　　　　Yards